LORD
MAKE ME
MORE
FRUITY

A Study of the Fruit of the Spirit

BY: JOAN GASPERSON

Published in Ocala, Florida by Joan Gasperson through Lulu Publishing

ISBN 978-0-578-06181-8

DEDICATION

I dedicate this book to the memory of my Father and Mother, Paul and Evelyn Coyle. Whose faithfulness to the Lord helped me to grow in love and service of Jesus Christ.

To my dear husband Bob, who was patient with me while I spent hours at the computer.

To my children, Darin and Terry. I am very proud of them.

Last but not least, my daughter-in-love, Tina, a splendid writer in her own right. She encouraged me and inspired me in my endeavor, and helped me in getting ready for publishing.

TABLE OF CONTENTS

INTRODUCTION

The inspiration for this book came to me one Sunday morning as I sat in choir. I can't say whether it was something the pastor had said or some-thing I had eaten that morning. Anyway there it was invading my mind. <u>Lord Make Me More Fruity.</u>

Wow! I am sure you are asking yourself, is she fruity or something? Read to find out.

The inspiration for this title came as a result of an experience I had years ago. We lived in Seminole, Florida at the time and were members of Calvary Baptist Church in Clearwater; where I was employed as the receptionist.

There was a young man that would come in the church office occasionally. He wasn't a member of our church. He appeared to be in his twenties, and sad to say not quite all there if you know what I mean.

He must have had a Catholic background, because each time he came in he would ask could he see the Father. I would explain to him each time; we did not have a father or priest, we had a pastor.

On the last encounter I had with him he gave the reason for his visit. He explained he had come because he wanted to know how he could become more fruity. I am ashamed to say that I had to bite my tongue to keep from laughing out loud, I was thinking young man you are fruity enough.

Of course the young man was talking about the Fruit of the Spirit found in Galatians 5:22-23 But the fruit of the Spirit is **love, joy, peace, patience, kindness, goodness, faith, gentleness, and self-control. Against such there is no law.**

The pastor was not in the office that day so he could not talk with him.

I do not remember what I said to the young man, but I am afraid he left not finding out how to be more fruity.

As I sat in choir that Sunday contemplating what the young man had said so many years ago, I came to the realization that many Christians do not realize that they have all of the fruit of the Spirit they are ever going to get, (in other words they are as fruity as they are going to get).

I felt inspired to write this book so that perhaps a new Christian can start out on the right foot or to help older Christians to grow in Spirit.

Chapter 1

THE SPIRIT----WHO?

The first thing in order is to define the source of the fruit. God's word tells us that apart from me you can do nothing. Jesus spent His last days on this earth preparing his disciples for what was to come. He told them to stay in Jerusalem until the Holy Spirit would come. He knew that in order for them to accomplish the great task ahead they would need far more than just personal experiences, they would need super natural power.

Jesus Christ was God in the flesh. He was not half man and half God; he was all man and all God. When He walked on this earth He was limited by time and space. He could not be everywhere at once. He told his disciples except I go away the Holy Spirit cannot come.

Who is the Holy Spirit? A lot of people speak of the Spirit as if He were not a person. Holy Spirit is not just an object, He is a person. He is the third person of the Trinity; God the Father, God the Son and God the Holy Spirit.

Many denominations refer to the Godhead as the trinity. Although you will not find the word trinity referred to in the Bible the concept is there.

The first introduction we have of the triune God is in Genesis 1:26, **God said let us make man in our image and after our likeness.** John 1:1 tells us that Christ was there and Genesis 1:2 tells us that the Spirit was there. So in the very beginning we see the presence of the triune God.

On the day Jesus was baptized, all three were present, the Spirit descended like a dove and rested upon Jesus, and the Father spoke from heaven saying **"this is my beloved Son in whom I am well pleased.'** (Mathew 3:16-17)

Now that it has been established who the Spirit is, let me try and explain what His purpose is. The Spirit represents the power and wisdom of God. He is omnipresent, that means he can be everywhere at once. We do not have to worry that Holy Spirit may be busy helping someone else and not have time for us. He can be with us and everyone else also.

In the Old Testament God's Spirit did not always stay with man. He would choose to abide with certain persons at certain times.

The Spirit of God led the children of Israel in a cloud by day and pillow of fire by night as they wandered through the wilderness to the promise land.

He came upon Saul when he was anointed king, and left him when he committed sin.

He rested on His prophets when the Father had a message for His people.

He was with David and although he sinned greatly, God's Spirit did not leave him because he admitted, confessed and repented of his sins.

In the New Testament we see the Spirit coming to stay with those who believe. On the day of Pentecost, God's Spirit came and filled each person seated in the room. They received a Holy boldness which they never had before. Once they cowered with fear, but with the Spirit's power they spoke with wisdom and boldness. As they spoke, men were convicted of their sin by the Spirit.

The Bible tells us that unless a person is drawn by the Spirit. He cannot be saved. The Spirit was sent to convict men of sin, of righteousness and judgment to come. (John 16:8-11)

Another attribute is that He is omnipotent. That means He is all powerful. There is not anything that He cannot do. In the Bible we read; with God all things are possible to those who believe. The reason this is possible is the Spirit lives and resides within us.

Another attribute is omniscience; this means that he knows everything. In I John 2:27 we are told that we have no need that any man teach us. God's Spirit can teach us all things because He knows all things.

Jesus said of the Spirit, **when He the Spirit of truth comes He will show you all things.** (John 16:13) There is no wisdom greater than His. He will give His wisdom to us, in James 1:5 it says, **"If any of you lack wisdom let him ask of God who gives to all men**

liberally. The Spirit is there to help us through any situation.

When we believe in Christ Jesus we are sealed by the Holy Spirit until the day of redemption. We do not receive a little of the Spirit now and a little later, as some denominations preach.

I heard a radio pastor say one time that we get a measure of the Holy Spirit which is contrary to what the Bible says. John 3:34 says: **"For He whom God sent speaks the Words of God, for God does not give the Spirit by measure.**

We have all of the Spirit that we will ever get. He promises never to leave us nor forsake us. He is with us at all times. He is there to help us, empower us, and guide us. Since He lives in us, His characteristics are ours also.

This brings us to the Fruit of the Spirit. Although you cannot have one without the other, I will take each attribute separately and explain what it should look like, so we can examine ourselves. The Bible says that by their fruit you will know them.

When we become Christians we become new creations in Christ Jesus, old things pass away and all things become new. (II Cor. 5:17) This does not mean that we become perfect but there is going to be a difference.

We are saved by grace and there is nothing that we can do to earn our salvation but that does not free us to continue to live as we lived before.

Jesus not only freed us from the penalty of sin; He freed us from the power of sin. A person who continues to live as he lived before, with no change whatsoever, needs to take a spiritual inventory.

We are told many times in the Bible to examine ourselves. Jesus said, **"not everyone who says unto me Lord, Lord shall enter into the kingdom,"** (Mathew 7:21) In I John 5:13 we read, **"These things I have written to you who believe in the name of the Son of God, that you may know that you have eternal life; and that you may continue to believe in the name of the Son of God.**

When a person has the Spirit he will produce fruit. This is where we become fruit inspectors. This little book will examine the fruit and hopefully help you see if the Spirit has produced His fruit in you.

QUESTIONS FOR CHAPTER 1

1. Who is the Holy Spirit?
2. What is His purpose?
3. Who has access to Him?
4. Can His power in our lives be limited? If so, how?
5. Have you given Him complete control over your life?

CHAPTER 2

LOVE

The first section of the fruit is love. In today's society this word is thrown around in reference to just about everything. i.e.: I love my job. I love my house. I love steak and potatoes. I love my dog. Is that what love is? What is love?

The Webster dictionary definition says: a feeling of strong or constant regard for and dedication to someone; to hold dear, to feel compassion, devotion, or tenderness towards.

We do not want to get our view of what love is from men but from God Himself.

The first thing we need to establish is love is not a feeling. Love can produce feelings but it in and of itself is not a feeling.

Of the Greek words available to describe love, Eros (sexual love) does not occur in the New Testament . Phileo, connoting natural affection, occurs some 25 times, with philadelphia (brotherly love) five times, and philia (friendship) only in James 4:4. Storge, connoting natural affection between relatives, appears occasionally in compounds.

By far the most frequent word is agape, generally assumed to mean moral goodwill that proceeds from esteem, principle, or duty rather than attraction of charm. Agape is very similar in meaning to hesed in that both denote dedication. Agape specifically means to love the undeserving, despite disappointment and rejection.

A closer look will be taken of three of these definitions

Eros from which we get erotic or sexual attraction, is where most of the world is today. Everywhere you turn whether TV, movies, books, internet or any other form of media you are bombarded with the sex issue.

What God intended as a beautiful experience for a married man and woman has become perverted, a butt for jokes, a deviation from what God intended.

There is much to be said about how the world has turned out in this area but that is not the purpose of this book so we will move on.

Next we have "phileo". This is defined as brotherly love, the kind of love that we have for our families and friends.

The type of love that we are referring to in this book is "agape". This word is best defined as godly love. How is God's love different? What is the measuring stick for us to know if we possess that kind of love?

The best definition of love is found in the Bible.

I Corinthians 13 is the best literary on love we could possibly find. Paul described love as follows:

1. **Love suffers long and is kind.** A person who possesses Godly love will be patient even in the midst of being hurt. They are kind to others even when they don't deserve it. They do not retaliate when wronged. They are more concerned with the needs of others than they are of their own. They are not quick to lash back and try to get even. They leave it in God's hands.
2. **Love does not envy.** This means that

we do not become all bent out of shape when others seem to be more blessed than we. We do not resent them because they are seemingly better off. We aren't jealous because of their success. We encourage them in their abilities and gifts. We do not become angry and resentful.

3. **<u>Love does not parade itself and is not puffed up.</u>** This person does not have to be in the limelight. They are not filled with pride. They don't think themselves better than other people just because perhaps God has chosen to use them in a particular way. They realize all gifts come from God and no gift is any better than another. All gifts have their purpose. They don't serve to get recognition for what they do.

4. **<u>Love does not behave rudely.</u>** We should exemplify Christ in all of our actions. We should be concerned with the feelings and needs of others. We should be courteous and considerate. Our purpose is to encourage and build up not tear down. We are to be careful

of what we say and how we say it.

5. **<u>Love does not seek it own.</u>** Our purpose in life should be what can we do for others not what can other people do for me. The "what's in for me attitude" does not belong in this type of love. We must be truly dead to self.

6. **<u>Love is not easily provoked.</u>** Most anger that people exhibit comes when we fail in the previous part. Most people get angry when they feel that their space has been violated. They take everything personally. It is you hurt me so I am going to hurt you attitude. A person who is filled with Godly love does not fly off the handle. They have self control in all situations. There are times that we need to get angry at sin and violence against others and the evil in the world. Jesus became angry at the things that were going on in the temple and drove out the money changers. He took action against that evil.

7. **<u>Love thinks no evil.</u>** We are not

always looking for the worse in others or finding something wrong with everything. Look for the good in everything, be positive.

8. **Love does not rejoice in iniquity but rejoices in the truth.** We are guided by the truth of God's word and we rejoice when that truth is followed. We hate evil and love good.

9. **Love bears all things, believes all things, hopes all things, and endures all things.** No matter what comes our way we are able to cope because we know who holds tomorrow. We trust in the power and promise of God's word. Knowing that all things work together for the good to those who love God.

This kind of love will never fail. It will remain in the good times and during the bad times. It is not dependent on outward circumstances.

There is much on love written in the Bible. All of creation was created so that God could love us and we could love God. He desires that intimate relationship with His children. **God commended His love towards us in that while we were yet sinners Christ died for us.** (Romans 5:8)

Genuine love comes not because the person or persons deserve it. Love is not just something that God does, God is love. He cannot not love, it is who is He is. It is His essence.

When we become one in Christ Jesus then that love is imparted to us. Jesus said in John 13:34-35; **A new commandment I give you: Love one another, as I have loved you, so you must love one another. By this all men will know that you are my disciples if you love one another.** It is a litmus test as to whether or not you are a Christian.

An excellent passage to read regarding love in the Christian life is I John. It is a must read for all Christians. Hate cannot live where there is love. That does not mean we have to like everyone, or like what they do. God hates sin but loves the sinner.

That is the reason Jesus went to the cross. God's holiness prevented Him from fellowshipping with sinners so He provided a means for us to be cleansed of sin. The nails did not keep Jesus on the cross love did. He could have stopped it at any time but His great love for us kept Him there. **Greater love has no man than this that a man lay down his life for a friend**. (John 15:13)

When the Pharisees came to Jesus, one of them being a lawyer, ask Jesus what was the greatest commandment. We find His answer in Mark 12:29-31; **The first of all commandments is, "Hear; O Israel, the Lord our God, the Lord is one. And you shall love the Lord your God with all your heart, with all your soul, with all your mind and with all your strength. This is the first commandment. "And the second like it is; you shall love your neighbor as yourself." There is no other commandment greater than these.**

Why did Jesus just give these two commandments? Aren't there many; especially those that are referred to as the Ten Commandments? He used these because if these two are kept then all the rest will be kept. If you love God with all your heart, soul, mind and strength you will know there is only one

God. He alone is to be worshiped. No one or anything is to come before your relationship to Him. You will honor Him. You will serve Him. He will have your complete allegiance. All that you are heart, soul, mind and strength.

Heart – This represents your emotions, affections, morality, moods, courage, and personality.

Soul – This is the real you, also referred to as your spirit. God formed man from the dust of the earth. Then He breathed into Him the breath of life and man became a living soul. Your spirit will live forever, either with God or separated from God.

Mind – This refers to your intellect, will, mental capacity to reason, think, and learn. You are able to determine right from wrong and choose which way you will go. It is often referred to as our conscience and our sub-conscience thoughts.

Strength – This represent the physical body.

Therefore, we are to love God with all that we are. Nothing held back. Jesus said that the second commandment was similar to it, "To love your neighbor as yourself."

When we keep this commandment, we will honor our parents, we will not murder, we will not commit adultery, we will not steal, we will not lie, and we will not covet what belongs to our neighbor.

This kind of love can only come by the power of the Holy Spirit. Without the Spirit, we tend to love ourselves more than anything. We are more concerned with what we want instead of what God wants or what others need from us.

When we are controlled by the Holy Spirit then His fruit of love will cause us to give our all to others.

We have a motto in our church that states what should be the goal of every Christian. It says, "Love God, Love People, Serve God by Serving People."

When we have Godly love this will be the controlling force in our lives. Our number one purpose in life will be to be obedient to all that He would have us do. He will have first place and in having first place it will cause us to love others as He loves them.

In concluding our chapter on love let us take one last look at I Corinthians 13. Paul emphasized the fact that without love everything else becomes useless. He also reminded us how that in the end all those things will pass away and only three things will last forever. These are faith, hope and love and he ended it by saying that the greatest of the three is love.

How can we have this kind of love? Those who believe in Jesus Christ and have received Him as their Lord and Savior have this love through the power of the Holy Spirit. We just need to submit to Him and allow His fruit to shine through. Love is of God and they who love are born of God.

QUESTIONS FOR CHAPTER 2

1. What are the different types of love?
2. Can you love someone even after that special feeling is gone?
3. What is the source of genuine love?
4. What is one of the evidences that you are a Christian?
5. What are the three things that outlast everything else? List in order of importance.

Chapter 3

JOY

The next section is Joy. Most people in today's society mistake being happy with having joy. This could not be further from the truth. Happiness is dependent upon circumstances. If things are going good then we are happy. If they are not then we are sad.

Joy is present during the good and the bad. Joy comes from within.

Although closely related in such ways as having a sense of wellbeing, comfort, excitement, enthusiasm, rejoicing, and delight; joy can be present when things around us are falling apart.

The Bible has much to say about the joy of the believer. All through its pages we are commanded to be filled with joy. It is God's word that brings us joy in crucial times.

The first reason for joy is; we are commanded to be filled with joy. Some of the many scriptures are as follows:

Ps 5:11 But let all who take refuge in you rejoice; let them ever sing for joy, and spread your protection over them, that those who love your name may exult in you.

Ps 32:11 Be glad in the Lord, and rejoice, O righteous, and shout for joy, all you upright in heart!

Ps 149:5 Let the godly exult in glory; let them sing for joy on their beds.

Col 1:11 May you be strengthened with all power, according to his glorious might, for all endurance and patience with joy,

Phil. 4:4 Rejoice in the Lord always, I will say it again. Rejoice.

It is God's will that we be filled with joy. Jesus said that the reason that He came was that our joy would be complete.

The New Testament writers gave their purpose for writing; so that our joy would be complete.

What do Christians have to rejoice about when things are in such turmoil? The economy, the government, finances, job issues, health issues, you name it things around us seem to be falling apart. Our world is rapidly changing from what we are accustomed.

Can we really be filled with joy in such circumstances? Here again we find our answers in the Bible.

Ps 92:4   For you, O Lord, have made me glad by your work; at the works of your hands I sing for joy.

We can rejoice because He created all things and He is in control of all things. Our lives are hidden in Him. We can see Him at work in everything and every situation. We don't have to fear what is happening in this world. All things are going according to His plan. We know the end of the story.

Luke 6:23   Rejoice in that day, and leap for joy, for behold, your reward is great in heaven.

We can rejoice even in persecution because we know our reward in heaven is greater.

James 1:2   Count it all joy, my brothers, when you meet trials of various kinds,

We can rejoice because we know that our difficulties come to help us grow in strength and courage. God promised that He would work everything out for good to all of us who are called according to His purpose. (Romans 8:28)

I remember an old song that talked about how little flowers grow. Sometimes rain must come in order for them to grow. So it is in the Christian's life. The storms of life cause us to grow in our Christian faith. We are never left alone in our difficulties. He has a purpose in them all.

John 16:24   Until now you have asked nothing in my name. Ask, and you will receive, that your joy may be full.

We can rejoice because we can ask anything in His name and He hears us. We can rejoice in our salvation. We can rejoice in our position in Christ Jesus.

We are children of God. We can trust Him to take care of us. He promised He would never leave us nor forsake us. We are not alone.

There are so many other things the Christians can rejoice in, the Bible is full of all His rich promises.

Why then are there so many Christians who seem to lack the joy that is ours in Christ Jesus? There could be many reasons for this but I will narrow it down to two specific ones.

The first is that not everyone that says they are a Christian is one. Jesus, himself said that many would come to Him in that day and say, **"have we not cast our devils in your name, and done many wonderful works in your name" and He will say depart from me because I do not know you**. (Math. 7:22-23) They have not been "born again". They know about Jesus but they do not know Him.

I remember Billy Graham saying one time that he believed that only 20% of the local church was born again.

There is only one way to God and that is Jesus Christ. Works will not get us there, belonging to a local church, being baptized, or trying to be good enough to get God's favor. It is sad but true, many church members do not experience joy, because they do not know the joy giver.

What about those who do know Him yet walk around with joyless lives? The result could be sin.

A good example of that was King David. He had committed adultery and murder. He tried to hide his sin but Nathan the prophet came to him and exposed his sin. David repented of his sin. In Psalm 51 we have his prayer of repentance. One of the verses says, **"restore unto me the joy of thy salvation."** He had lost his joy because of sin in his life.

Many Christians are living with un-confessed sin. Or they are out of the will of God. We cannot experience the joy of the Lord if there is sin in our life, whether it is omission or commission.

We experience joy when our delight is in the Lord and we do His will. Joy comes to the believer when he is totally and completely committed to God and His purpose.

Many Christians are living joyless and unproductive lives because they have lost their first love. Come back to your first love and renew your relationship with Him. Our heavenly Father desires to give us the best. He wants us to be joyful. He wants us to be free from the worry and cares of this life. We can live in victory and joy but He must have first place.

QUESTIONS FOR CHAPTER 3

1. What is the definition of joy?
2. Can we experience joy when things go wrong?
3. Why do a lot of Christians not experience this joy?
4. What are some of the things that keep us from experiencing joy?
5. What do we need to do to have this kind of joy?

Chapter 4

PEACE

The word peace occurs 348 times in the Bible, but what is peace?

In today's society the definition of peace would be the absence of war. The peace mentioned in Galatians does not fall into that definition, although both types of peace will be covered in these pages.

First to be covered is the absence of war. This kind of peace does not exist in our world today.

Everywhere we turn we see conflict of one kind or another. Government leaders are always talking about peace and some even make false claims to appease the masses. All you have to do is look around.

James in his letter covered this subject quite well.

What is the source of the wars and the fights among you? Don't they come from the cravings that are at war within you? 2 You

desire and do not have. You murder and covet and cannot obtain. You fight and war.

From the beginning, after the fall of man war has existed. There have been conflicts among individuals, and families; and certainly not least conflicts among nations. James gave the reason for all the warring and hatred. It is man's lust for what he cannot have. We lust after what we cannot have and will do anything to have what we want. The human race cannot stand the fact that someone may be better off than themselves

Man is inherently evil. Jeremiah said, **"The human heart is deceitful above all things and desperately wicked."** (Jer. 17:9)

Satan entices the heart of man to take what is not his. Man easily falls for his deceit. There has never been a time that there has not been a war somewhere. Solomon experienced a time of peace, but that does not mean that the nations around him did not war. Jesus said that we would always have wars until His coming.

 Mathew 24: 6 You are going to hear of wars and rumors of wars. See that you are not

alarmed, because these things must take place, but the end is not yet.

7 For nation will rise up against nation, and kingdom against kingdom. There will be famines and earthquakes in various places.

These events are descriptive of what will happen up until Jesus sets up His reign on this earth.

All around us we hear the cry for peace. This is just another fulfillment of prophecy.

I Thessalonians 5:3 When they say, "Peace and security" then sudden destruction comes on them, like labor pains on a pregnant woman,

There will be no peace until Jesus comes. Sinful man will always fight and make war. It is his nature. The Bible tells us that it is going to get worse and worse not better as some would have us believe.

What about the Christian? Can we live in peace?

This brings us to the peace spoken of in Galatians. The type of peace you can receive even during times of turmoil and strife, the peace that passes all understanding by all human standards. It can be defined as tranquility, quiet rest, calm, a sense of security and well-being.

Jesus before He ascended back into heaven assured us of this kind of peace.

John 14:27   Peace I leave with you; my peace I give to you. Not as the world gives do I give to you. Let not your hearts be troubled, neither let them be afraid.

After reading these verses, we also could add the absence of fear and worry as a definition for peace.

Many people live in constant worry and fear. They worry about not only what is occurring but what might happen. They allow fear to keep them from accomplishing all that God would have them. Jesus says not to allow this to happen. There is no need to worry or fret because Jesus is in control. He takes care of all His children.

I know a young woman that was a best friend to my daughter when she was growing up. This young woman has not left her house for years. She is bound by anxiety about getting out into public. She was not this way when she was younger. I do not know what has caused her to get into this state. One thing I do know, Jesus says that we do not have to live like this. When we live in His power we don't have to fear.

I John 4:18 There is no fear in love; but perfect love casts out fear: because fear hath torment. He that fears is not made perfect in love

Jesus came to give us peace and contentment. He told us to lay all of our cares upon Him because He cares for us.(I Peter 5:7) When a person lives in fear he or she is not putting their trust in Jesus. The Bible tells us to trust in Him with all our hearts and not to be troubled by how we see or understand things. (Proverbs 3:5) We are to acknowledge Him and seek His power to overcome.

He is able to remove our fears and anxieties. All of us at times get nervous and concerned but when we claim God's word then we can have that peace that passes understanding.

Very few Christians know what vast resources are available in the Bible because they never read it. They look at God's word as some archaic ancient book that has little to do with them. Little do they know that in its pages lies the secret to a full and meaningful life. It is food for the soul, it can enrich and enhance our lives in greater ways than any other book.

I am involved in a business that encourages us to read motivational books. This is a good habit to form. Much can be gained by reading such books but there is no greater motivational book than the Holy Bible. It is the only book that if you follow all that is said within its pages it will make you a new person from the inside out.

When we know the Word and are directed by it we can obtain the peace we are speaking of in these texts.

Are you troubled in your spirit? Look to the Word. Allow the Spirit to enrich your life.

There is no need for a Christian to be in distress. We are human, there will be times and circumstances that cause us stress but that stress can be overcome when we place our trust in Him.

We do not have to live in fear and worry. Here again we gain strength from the Word.

Ps. 29:11 The Lord gives His people strength, the Lord blesses His people with peace.

People search for peace in many ways and places. They try to masked fear and worries with drugs. They think if they obtain great riches then they will have peace. They search and search and search but they never find it because they are looking in all the wrong places.

Is. 26:3 You will keep in perfect peace the mind that is dependent on you for it is trusting in you.

If you want peace submit to the Spirit that is in you because He desires to give you peace.

We haven't even begun to scratch the service of what God has to say about peace. There is so much more that could be written. You can find it in the Bible. Study it.

QUESTIONS FOR CHAPTER 4

1. What is peace?
2. Where can we find peace?
3. Is peace the absence of troubles?
4. Why is it important to know what God's word has to say about peace?
5. Are you living in peace or are you controlled by worry and fear?

Chapter 5

PATIENCE

We all have heard the old adage, "don't ever pray for patience." Why is that? This probably comes from the fact that the Bible says "tribulations bring patience." (James 1:3)Therefore people think if they pray for patience that troubles will come.

Although the Bible does contain these words; that does not mean that in order to get patience we have to go through hardships. We already possess patience in the fruit of the Spirit. We just need to allow the Spirit to work through us to produce this patience.

If we look around at society today, we do not see a lot of patience. Everyone is use to having everything in an instant. Instant coffee, instant soup, fast food restaurants, instant car washes, microwave ovens, high speed internet; we could go on and on.

We don't like to wait on anything. We experience road rage because people are in such a hurry they don't want to yield to anyone or anything. We could describe it this way, "it is a me, me, me, now, now, now society."

We need to look at what patience really means. A summary of the definition found in the MW Collegiate could go a follows:

The ability to remain calm, cool, and collected even in the midst of difficult times.

A person who possesses patience is a person who without complaining or bickering can go through whatever comes his way. They don't blame others. They are able to deal with the problem.

Paul the apostle exhibited patience in his epistle to the Philippians 4.

11 I don't say this out of need, for I have learned to be content in whatever circumstances I am. 12 I know both how to have a little, and I know how to have a lot. In any and all circumstances I have learned the secret [of being content]—whether well-fed or hungry, whether in abundance or in need

This does not mean that Paul was happy with every situation that he experienced. It meant that his hope rested in Jesus Christ and he knew that everything would work out as the Lord wanted it to, for the good.

He was not always complaining with a woe is me attitude

Recall the story when he was in jail in Philippi. (Acts 16). He and Silas, although in a cold, dark dungeon in chains, sang songs and praised God. Paul's purpose was too great to waste time complaining and being impatient.

Solomon, the wisest man that ever lived expressed it this way;

Proverbs 14:29 A patient person [shows] great understanding, but a quick-tempered one promotes foolishness.

A person who is patient thinks before he acts or speaks. He calmly reasons out each situation. He waits before he reacts.

An impatient person flies off the handle and does things that he often regrets in the long term. He takes everything personally and blames everyone else for his troubles.

This type person is often referred to as an A type individual. He is always uptight, to the point that it can even affect his health.

A patient person is most often a healthy person. He is able to stop and analyze a situation and come up with a better solution. There is less conflict around patient people. They are better able to handle the situation.

The tribulations that they experience just tend to make them stronger. They do not allow circumstances to get them down. They have learned as the apostle Paul did that God is in control and the Lord will take care of them.

James summed it up well when he said;

James 1:2 My brethren count it all joy when you fall into various trials, 3 knowing that the trying of your faith produces patience. 4 But let patience have its perfect work, that you may be perfect and complete, lacking nothing.

The ultimate goal of patience is perfection.

QUESTIONS FOR CHAPTER 5

1. What is patience?
2. Do we have to go through tribulations to get patience?
3. What happens when a person is impatient?
4. What are the rewards of being patient?
5. Why is patience seemly so much more difficult than the other fruit sections?

Chapter 6

KINDNESS

Kindness the state of being that includes the attributes of loving affection, sympathy, friendliness, pleasantness, gentleness, and goodness.

A person who is kind is more concerned with the feelings and concerns of the other person more than he is himself.

They have the ability to make people feel at ease in any situation. Their tenderness is felt in the way they treat people.

They have the ability to make others feel at ease. They are not judgmental. They have the ability to forgive others for past wrongs. They share in their sorrows and their gladness.

The Bible tells us to be kind to one another, and to forgive one another just as our Savior has forgiven us. (Ephesians 4:32)

Kindness can be revealed in two ways.

One way is through our actions. When we see a person in need, if we have it within our power we supply that need or we find a way to meet that need. We cannot just look the other way. We show compassion towards them.

Sometimes a simple hug could do wonders for someone who is lonely and discouraged.

Another way to show kindness is to care for a young couple's children that have no family.

 I know many years ago when our children were young and we lived away from grandparents. Our church family reached out to us and cared for our children many times.

Other times they have helped us move. I do not know what we would have done if it had not been for these Christian brothers and sisters, who gave of themselves, and showed us kindness.

There are many ways we can show kindness. All we need to do is look around, especially during these hard times.

Another way of showing kindness is through our speech. Our words can build up or they can tear down.

A soft answer often turns away anger and bitterness. Where there is no fuel for the fire it goes out. Words once spoken can never be taken back. We need to think before we speak. James described the tongue as a flaming fire that no one can control. He said that the person who could control his tongue was perfect. (James 3)

How many children's wills have been broken because of ridiculing words? Words such as; you are stupid, you will never amount to anything. A child will model what he sees and hears.

When a person is kind, he will use words of encouragement. He will build up and not tear down.

Kindness will not only benefit the receiver of the kindness but the giver of kindness will benefit also.

Proverbs 11:17   A man who is kind benefits himself, but a cruel man hurts himself.

Proverbs 21:21 The one who pursues righteousness and kindness, will find life, righteousness, and honor

Let kindness rule in your hearts. Show compassion and understanding to all those around you. In this way you will reflect Jesus.

QUESTIONS FOR CHAPTER 6

1. What is kindness?
2. What are the two ways to show kindness?
3. Who benefits from showing kindness?
4. Describe some acts of kindness?
5. Do you react to others in kindness?

Chapter 7

GOODNESS

Goodness comes from the root word "good". Webster's collegiate dictionary defines good as; favorable character, sound, agreeable, pleasant, and reliable.

We can look at the word in two different ways. The first way we can look at the word is as a state of doing. There are many people in this world who do "good" things. Many are involved in charitable organizations that help others that are in need. Civic clubs do things which better the community. Often we hear of celebrities who are involved in different causes to help better others.

When a child is missing volunteers spend hours searching for the child.

There are people who are active in what they think will better society. This is not bad. We as occupants of this world should be concerned about making it a better place for ourselves and others.

It is the other aspect of good with which our study is concerned, the state of being.

Does doing good, make a person good?

Let's consider the fiction story of "Robin Hood". Everyone knows that story from childhood. What was it that he did? He robbed from the rich and gave to the poor. His desire to give to the poor was indeed good. His method of getting that done was evil. He was not a good person because he was a thief. The fact that he gave it to the poor did not change the truth.

The Biblical answer to the previous question is no. The Bible tells us that there is none that is good no not one. Jesus said; **there is none good but one, that is, God. (Mark 10:18b)** No matter how much good we may do, it will not make us good. There are many people who think that when we stand in the judgment God is going to weigh our good deeds against our bad deeds. Then if our good outweighs our bad then we are going to be allowed into heaven. Let me set the record straight. The Bible tells us in Eph. 2:8-9;

For by grace you are saved, through faith and that not of yourself; it is a gift of God not of works, lest anyone should boast.

We don't get to heaven by doing good we get to heaven by being good. How can we be good? Didn't I just say there is none good but God? You are correct.

This is the reason God the Father sent His Son to earth so we can be made righteous. For by His grace and mercy we are made right with God. When God looks at a person who has received His Son, He does not see our sin. Our sins have been covered by the blood of His righteousness. Therefore we are made good in Christ Jesus.

What does it mean for us to be good or righteous in the spiritual sense?

Let's look at a life that is characterized in Jesus. In the spiritual sense a person is well founded in the principles and will of the Lord. We give of ourselves unconditionally, not for what it can get us but what it can give others. A Christian should be a person of character and of a good reputation. Well grounded in the truth of God's word and for what it stands. One who is reliable and can be trusted.

Ephesians 2:10 goes on to say that we are saved to do good works. Although we are not saved by our good works, once we are saved we will do good works.

We will be concerned with how other persons see us. We will do our best to live lives that are blameless. Paul dealt with this issue in **I Corinthians 8**. He was discussing what was right and wrong for the Christian.

There are some things that are not necessarily wrong but if we indulge in it would hurt someone else. Paul said if eating meat offends my brother then I will not eat meat. Eating the meat was not wrong but if someone else was hurt by it he would not do it.

We as God's children have a responsibility to act in ways that will bring honor and glory to Him. Our old natures have been changed we are made new. Our purpose should be to reflect the goodness of God.

We have that power through the Holy Spirit.

QUESTIONS FOR CHAPTER 7

1. Can the believer be good?
2. What are some examples of goodness?
3. What is the source of our goodness?
4. Where do we learn what we should do?
5. What are the two areas that **good can be explained?**

Chapter 8

FAITHFUL

The next section of fruit is faithful.

In **I Corinthians. 4:2** we are told that it is a requirement that we be faithful. What does it mean to be faithful?

Webster's dictionary defines faithful as being firm in adherence and observance of duty; steadfast, true to the facts.

Perhaps if we take a look at some synonyms for faithful it will help us better understand what it means to be faithful.

Loyal – a person who is loyal will not be easily tempted to leave the foundation on which his faith is built. He will be strong in his beliefs, not easily swayed.

Ephesians 4:14, that we should no longer be children, tossed to and fro and carried about with every wind of doctrine, by the trickery of men, in the cunning craftiness of deceitful plotting, 15 but, speaking the truth

in love, may grow up in all things into Him who is the head—Christ—

He will hold true to the teaching of the Bible. He will search for himself the truth. The Spirit in him will help him to be able to discern between the truth and a lie. He will be firm in what he believes and in whom he believes.

He will not be tempted by every new idea and thought that comes along.

Steadfast - to be firm in your love, allegiance, and conviction. No one or anything will be able to move you. You are not subject to change.

There are some things that need to change, not all change is bad. The steadfast person will weigh each change carefully in accordance with God's word.

Some of the changes that have occurred in the modern day church are not necessarily good.

A good measure would be; does it lift up Jesus? Does it line up with worldly standards or Biblical standards?

I fear that in a lot of churches the change has been so great that you cannot tell the difference in the church and a social club.

A church or individual that is filled with the Spirit will be steadfast and unmovable. Their main purpose will be to spread the gospel message to a lost and dying world. Anything short of that is just a social club.

Resolute - a strong resolve and determination to hold true to the purpose of Christ.

A good example is Daniel and the three Hebrew children. We are told in the book of Daniel that they resolved not to be defiled by the king's meat. They refused even in the face of death to turn from what they believed. God rewarded their faithfulness.

Later on in Daniel the three Hebrew children were tossed in the fiery furnace because they were unwilling to bow their knees to another god. God delivered them.

I could give many examples even up to modern day of men and women who remain faithful even unto death.

Faithful can also be described in another way. Rearrange it and you have full of faith.

What is faith? **Hebrews 11:1 says; faith is the substance of things hoped for the evidence of things not seen.**

The person who is full of faith will trust in God for all things. He will know that in Christ all things are possible.

Jesus said that if we have faith as small as a mustard seed we could remove mountains.

How often do we limit God from working in our lives because we just don't have the faith that He will do what He says He will do.

A prime example would be the story of when Jesus visited his own home town. The Bible tells us that he was unable to do many miracles because of their unbelief.

Our God is a big God. Nothing is impossible with Him.

The Bible says that faith comes by hearing and hearing by the word of God. (Romans 10:17)

What are some ways that a Christian can be faithful?

A Christian should be faithful in:

Church attendance - We all know that the church is not a building. We who believe and trust in Jesus Christ are the church.

We are referred to as the body of Christ. Each of us is members in particular. The Bible tells us that God has given each of us a gift to be used in the body.

How are these gifts to be used?

They are be used when the church gathers together.

Many persons have become disillusioned by the "institutionalized" church. They have in essence separated themselves from any semblance of what is called the church today.

I admit that most of the groups that call themselves a church leave a lot to be desired. Does that mean we should stop meeting together as the body of Christ? Absolutely not.

We need to look at what God's word has to say about this.

Hebrews 10:19 Therefore, brethren, having boldness to enter the Holiest by the blood of Jesus, 20 by a new and living way which He consecrated for us, through the veil, that is,

His flesh, 21 and having a High Priest over the house of God, 22 let us draw near with a true heart in full assurance of faith, having our hearts sprinkled from an evil conscience and our bodies washed with pure water. 23 Let us hold fast the confession of our hope without wavering, for He who promised is faithful. 24 And let us consider one another in order to stir up love and good works, 25 not forsaking the assembling of ourselves together, as is the manner of some, but exhorting one another, and so much the more as you see the Day approaching.

I don't know how it could get any plainer. I have heard some people say that to use this passage as evidence that we should meet together is being taken out of context.

If you read the whole chapter, you will see how Jesus' replaced the old sacrificial and priestly order because He himself is our high priest. His sacrifice has made us complete. There is no need for any further sacrifice. We can come boldly to the throne of grace. His truth is written in our hearts because we have believed. Then it goes on to say because of this we should remain faithful and continue in His word. We should grow in faith and trust, remaining faithful to His calling. Helping and encouraging our brothers and sisters to grow also.

These verses challenge us not only to continue to gather together but to do so more than ever. Why? Because the times are getting worse and worse and we need one another.

Also, the Lord Jesus' return is just around the corner.

This does not mean that we have to meet in big fancy churches with tall steeples. They are just buildings. Some of the churches meet in homes, some in store fronts, others in the out of doors, others in church buildings.

The main thing is that we meet together. Why? So the work of the church can be accomplished.

What is the work of the church?

Some would have you believe that the work of the church is to worship God. This could not be further from the truth.

It is true that we should worship God and only God. When we meet together it should be a culmination of our walk with Him during the week.

I believe that when people come together on Sunday and have giving very little thought to Him all week their worship becomes vain. The Father concerning the Israelites and their empty worship said, "I hate your solemn assemblies." (Amos 5:21) Why? They were honoring Him with their lips but their hearts were far from Him. He told him that God desired obedience over sacrifice (I Samuel 15:22-23)

We worship and honor God by what we do.

The purpose of the church is to spread the gospel message to those who have never heard and to build up and edify the body of Christ.

God has given each of us gifts, so that we can accomplish this goal.

Another reason is so that we can carry out the great commission of Christ in Mathew 28.

18 All authority has been given to Me in heaven and on earth. 19 Go, therefore, and

make disciples of all nations, baptizing them in the name of the Father and of the Son and of the Holy Spirit, 20 teaching them to observe everything I have commanded you. And remember, I am with you always, to the end of the age."

We, the church, as we are going, are to make disciples. Then we are to teach them all that Jesus has taught us. How can this be done, if we do not come together?

I have seen many people in my day who have become disillusioned with the "local" church, and have separated themselves. It has been my observation that they tend to lose their fervor for the Lord. Where once they had served faithfully, they now barely have time for Him. Instead of growing closer to God they seem to be drifting further away.

We need each other to encourage one another, to help one another carry out the great commission.

If you are involved in a group meeting and the great commission is not being carried out whether you are in a large church or a small group. Then you are not doing what you are supposed to be doing. If you are not growing in your faith and service then something is wrong and a change needs to be made.

Remember the Bible says that we are required to be faithful. Are you faithful?

QUESTIONS FOR CHAPTER 8

1. What is the requirement for stewards?
2. What does it mean to be faithful?
3. Can we be faithful apart from the local church?
4. What is the purpose of the church?
5. Are you carrying out the Great Commission?

CHAPTER 9

GENTLENESS

The root word of gentleness is gentle. When a person is gentle, he is not easily provoked. He is not quick to render harsh judgment. He is tender and understanding, willing to forgive.

Gentleness is one of God's major characteristics. He does not reward us according to our iniquities but is merciful. Jesus said of Himself that He was gentle and lowly in heart. (**Mathew 11:29**) We are to be like Him in all that we say and do.

We are given some guidelines in how we are to respond in gentleness.

The Living Bible paraphrases Solomon's words in Proverbs 15:4;

Gentle words are the tree of life, but a deceitful tongue crushes the spirit.

How many times have parents crushed the spirits of their children with harsh words, or spouses to one another?

A person who is characterized by gentleness with be slow to speak and quick to listen, and slow to get angry. **(James 1:19).**

Peter gave some instructions to the women in his epistle. Women may not always like what Peter and Paul have to say about them. If we are to be women of character and godliness we do well to listen to them.

I Peter 3:4 but let your adorning be the hidden person of the heart with the imperishable beauty of a gentle and quiet spirit, which in God's sight is very precious

The women that read this would do well to read the whole chapter of 1 Peter 3. It speaks of how a woman should dress, how we should act, and what should be important in her life.

Are these things important? You better believe they are. I think it is sad that in today's world is difficult to tell the difference between those who profess Christ and those who don't.

Does that mean we need to belittle and berate those who are guilty? Of course not, that is what being gentle is about.

We are told in Galatians 6:1 that **if we see someone who is overtaken in a fault to seek to restore them in a spirit of gentleness and meekness..** That is what a Christian mentor is all about, helping a person to grow in the faith so that the Holy Spirit can work to mold and shape them into the image of Christ Jesus. The best way we can help our fellow Christians is to live a life of gentleness and peace. A life that reflects Jesus Christ in all that we say and do.

Lest you men think that I have let you off the hook. I want to share with you what Paul has to say to fathers.

Ephesians 6:4 Fathers, don't exasperate your children by coming down hard on them. Take them by the hand and lead them in the way of the Master.

Sometimes fathers can be the worse in the area of gentleness. They live with the thought that's women's work. The man thinks he is weak if he exhibits gentleness.

Men all you need to do is look at your example, Jesus Christ. He was gentle, meek and lowly of heart, but He exhibited power and authority.

Fathers have a great influence upon their children for good or bad. Children live what they see at home.

Many younger fathers have learned to spend time with their children because they feel their fathers failed in this area. Spending time with our children is great, but what are we teaching our children during the time we spend with them? Do they see Jesus in everything we do? Are we exemplifying Jesus?

God challenged His people to teach their children diligently. They were to instruct them in the ways of the Lord, when they rose up, when they were eating, when they walked by the way.

In other words, they were to use every opportunity to tell them of God's love.

How tragic it will be if we spend time here on this earth with our kids but do not get to spend time in heaven because we never took the time to introduce them to Jesus. The example that you set as a father is very important.

How often does a son become an abuser if the father is one?

Fathers one of the best things that you can do for your children is to love their mother.

Colossians 3:19 challenges men to love their wives and not to be bitter against them.

We all have a great and awesome responsibility, not only to our physical families, but our spiritual families also.

Learn to live with a peaceable, quiet and gentle spirit.

QUESTIONS FOR CHAPTER 9

1. Is gentleness a sign of weakness in a man?
2. From where do we get our example of gentleness?
3. What are some ways we can show gentleness?
4. What is our greatest responsibility?
5. Do you have that gentle spirit?

CHAPTER 10

SELF-CONTROL

This brings us to the last section of the fruit of the Spirit. Of all the other parts, this is probably the most difficult to exhibit. We are often good at trying to control others but when it comes to ourselves, we have a tough opponent.

The definition is simple and plain, being in control of yourself.

Some examples of self-control will better help us understand what it means to be in control of oneself.

A person who is self-controlled is a disciplined person. They have everything in order. Their conduct is impeccable. The disciplined person knows what is expected of him and does it.

The self-controlled person is not slave to any addiction. Whether it is drugs, alcohol, the list could go on and on. Anything that controls you, whether good or bad, becomes your Lord..

A person who has himself under control will better be able to exhibit the other parts of the fruit of the Spirit. All of these come when in actuality we are controlled by the Spirit of God.

It is the Spirit who gives life, hope and peace. When we live in and through Him, all things are possible.

QUESTIONS FOR CHAPTER 10

1. What does it mean to have self-control?
2. How can we have self-control?
3. Who ultimately need to control us?
4. Can a person be saved and not have the Spirit?
5. Who or what controls your life?

CHAPTER 11

CHALLENGE

In these short few pages I have tried to explain in plain simple English what it means to be filled with the Holy Spirit.

I believe that a person who truly knows Christ will exhibit His fruit in their lives.

A person who is constantly filled with hate, despair, meanness, lack of joy, bad habits, unfaithfulness, harshness, and lack of control in their lives does not have the Spirit of God living within them.

This does not mean that we are perfect. There are times that we will fail. Circumstances tend to distract us at times. When we fail to stay in the Word and prayer, or fail to stay in sweet fellowship with believers, we grow weak. The Holy Spirit will not allow us to stay in that state.

He is here to convict us of sin, of righteousness and the judgment to come.

He is here to guide and defend us. He is here to teach us.

The Holy Spirit's purpose is to help we who are Christians to be all that we can be in Christ Jesus. We are not alone.

I challenge you to walk according to the precepts of God's word. Life will be a whole lot better if you do.

ABOUT THE AUTHOR

I am a wife of 42 years and mother of 2 grown children, 5 grandchildren and 5 great grandchildren with 1 on the way.

I do not have a degree but have many years experience in teaching God's word. I began teaching when I was thirteen years old.

I was born in Cowpens, SC to a humble Christian home.

I feel like the prophet Jeremiah when he said in my mother's womb you knew me and called me to be a prophet to the nations. Two weeks before I was born my Father received Jesus as his savior. I feel the Lord was giving me what I needed to serve Him.

My Father was a Southern Baptist minister for over 50 years. I grew up in a home that loved Jesus and taught me to love Him.

I received Jesus at the tender age of 5. I feel he has always had His hand on my life and love Him with all my heart.

In years past I often would listen to persons who had received Jesus in later years and would envy their amazing testimonies of Christ's deliverance.

One such time while I was contemplating this and bemoaning the fact that my testimony did not have the flare that some did. My Lord spoke to me and said, "Joan, I did deliver you from drugs, alcohol and all the other bad things. You just never experienced it. Praise the Lord for His infinite mercy. Except for the grace of God there go I.

It is because of this that I try to share the riches of God's word. It has been my guide and mainstay for many years.

I believe that God has graced me with knowledge of His word. Through such means as my own study, my Father and Mother, and the many wonderful pastors and teachers that I have had through the years, I have gained much insight.

I am no theologian; I have had no formal education other than high school. I am sure there are many who could have produced a much greater and more eloquent writing.

Somehow I feel that God wanted me to write this simple explanation of this beloved passage. If it can help one person, it will be worth it all. I hope you are blessed by it.

REFERENCES

Elwell, Walter A.;   Comfort, Philip Wesley:
Tyndale Bible Dictionary. Wheaton, Ill. :
Tyndale House Publishers, 2001 (Tyndale
Reference Library), S. 827

The New King James Version. Nashville :

Thomas Nelson, 1982, S.

The Holy Bible : Holman Christian
Standard Version. Nashville : Holman Bible
Publishers, 2003, S

The Holy Bible : English Standard Version.
Wheaton : Standard Bible Society, 2001, S.

Peterson, Eugene H.: The Message : The
Bible in Contemporary Language. Colorado
Springs, Colo. : NavPress, 2002, S.

www.ingramcontent.com/pod-product-compliance
Lightning Source LLC
Chambersburg PA
CBHW051044030426
42339CB00006B/195